MACMILLAN READERS

PRE-INTERMEDIATE LEVEL

Nelson Mandela

by Carl W Hart

Founding Editor: John Milne

The Macmillan Readers provide a choice of enjoyable reading materials for learners of English. The series is published at six levels – Starter, Beginner, Elementary, Pre-intermediate, Intermediate and Upper.

Level Control

Information, structure and vocabulary are controlled to suit the students' ability at each level.

The number of words at each level:

Starter	about 300 basic words
Beginner	about 600 basic words
Elementary	about 1100 basic words
Pre-intermediate	about 1400 basic words
Intermediate	about 1600 basic words
Upper	about 2200 basic words

Vocabulary

Some difficult words and phrases in this book are important for understanding the story. Some of these words are explained in the story, some are shown in the pictures, and others are marked with a number like this: …[3]. Words with a number are explained in the Glossary at the end of the book.

Answer Keys

Answer Keys for the *Points for Understanding* and *Exercises* sections can be found at www.macmillanenglish.com/readers

Audio Download

There is an audio download available for this title.
Visit www.macmillanenglish.com/readers for more information.

Contents

	The Places In This Story	4
1	A Divided Country	5
2	Troublemaker	8
3	The African National Congress	12
4	Action!	18
5	Banned	22
6	The Freedom Charter and the Treason Trial	27
7	Nomzamo Winifred Madikizela	32
8	The Sharpeville Massacre	35
9	Spear of the Nation	38
10	Robben Island	40
11	The Fight Continues	43
12	Free Mandela!	50
13	Last Steps	57
14	The Whole World Watches	61
	Points for Understanding	63
	Glossary	66
	Exercises	71

The Places In This Story

1

A Divided Country

Nelson Mandela was born into a divided country. The rulers[1] of South Africa were white people whose ancestors[2] came from Europe. They came to the country only a few hundred years earlier but the ancestors of the black majority[3] had lived in South Africa for thousands of years.

The Dutch were the first Europeans to live in South Africa. They arrived at the Cape of Good Hope in 1652. The Cape was a trading post[4]. Dutch ships could stop there for fresh food and water. The people who lived in the area were called Hottentots and Bushmen. The Dutch wanted the Hottentots to work for them, but the Hottentots refused[5]. So the Dutch brought prisoners and slaves[6] from Asia to work for them.

Soon more white people came. They wanted to live in the country and become farmers, or *boers*, as they are called in Dutch. At first the Africans shared the land. But more white people came and they wanted more and more land. When the Europeans took land they expected to keep it forever. The Boers sometimes caught Africans to make them slaves. The Africans fought the Boers, but they could not win against European weapons[7].

In the early 1800s, the British took over the Cape from the Dutch. The British liked the warm weather and the good land for farming. Soon they were coming in large numbers. The Boers were not happy about this. The British had a different language and different ideas. The British made slavery illegal[8] and gave equal rights[9] to non-whites. This made the Boers angry. In 1836, thousands of Boers gathered their slaves, cattle and sheep and moved north. They wanted to escape the British. During the journey, the Boers fought many battles with the African tribes[10]. The Xhosa, Sotho and Zulu all tried to stop them, but they only had spears and clubs[11]. The Boers had guns. In one fight, three thousand Zulus were killed near a river. Today that river is called Blood River.

Boer soldiers on Spion Kop, Ladysmith, in the early 1900s

The Boers moved north of the British and founded two independent countries, Transvaal and the Orange Free State. The Boers did not think of themselves as Dutch anymore. They were 'Afrikaners,' they said, 'the white tribe of Africa'.

In the beginning, the British were not interested in the Afrikaners. That changed when diamonds and gold were found in the late 1800s. Between 1880 and 1902, the British and Boers fought two wars. But Britain had more weapons and its army was more powerful. In 1910, the Union of South Africa became one country and a part of the British Empire[12]. Before the war, the British promised that all black Africans would be able to vote. However, the new British leaders only gave votes to blacks living in the Cape. And most of these blacks could not take part in elections. Only white people could do that. So blacks in the Cape could vote – but only for white people. And many blacks in the rest of South Africa could not vote at all.

In 1912, the African National Congress (ANC) was created[13] to help black people. But blacks continued to lose their rights. In 1913, a law was created which said that blacks could only buy land in certain areas of the country. That created a problem for the white government because they did not want blacks living in white areas. But they also needed blacks to work in the country's gold and diamond mines[14].

So the Government created a pass system[15] to control the movement of blacks inside South Africa. The passes allowed blacks to travel from their home to their workplace. But they could not travel anywhere else in the country. Blacks were no longer free to travel in their own land. They could live only in black-only 'townships' where the land was not good. They had no running water, telephones or electricity.

This system was later called 'apartheid', the Afrikaner word for 'apartness'. This was the world Nelson Mandela was born into. This was the world that Nelson Mandela would change.

7

2

Troublemaker

The 18th of July 1918 was a happy day in the small village of Mvezo in the Transkei region of South Africa. Gadla Henry Mphakanyiswa was a happy man. His wife, Nosekeni Fanny, was the mother of a new baby boy. The people of the village were happy for him and Nosekeni. Gadla was a respected[16] man from an important family. He had an important job. He was the chief[17] of the village of Mvezo and an adviser[18] to the king of the Thembu tribe. Gadla's connection to the royal house was strong. His great-grandfather was a king and he had also helped his nephew Jongintaba become the present king. Jongintaba never forgot that he owed Gadla a favour. One day he would return that favour.

The baby was named Rolihlahla. In the Xhosa language the name means 'pulling the branch of a tree', but it can also mean 'troublemaker'. It was a good name for the boy because one day he would make a lot of trouble.

Rolihlahla's sisters called the baby 'Buti'. Buti's father Gadla was also a troublemaker. He was a fair man and also a proud man. Because of this he had to make a difficult decision. Gadla was the chief of his village and he had to obey[19] King Jongintaba. However, the real power in South Africa was held by the white government and Gadla also had to obey the local white magistrate[20]. One day, Gadla refused to obey the magistrate. He wanted to do the right thing for his people.

The magistrate was angry, and he removed Gadla from the position of chief. Gadla was an important man in the Thembu tribe but there was nothing he could do. Even his nephew, the King, could not help him.

So Gadla lost his money and his important position in Mvezo. The family moved to Qunu, a small village north of Mvezo. In Qunu, Nosekeni's friends and family helped her and young Buti. Life was now more difficult but Buti had learnt an important lesson from his father. Gadla decided to do the right thing instead of the easy thing. One day Buti would make the same decision as his father.

Qunu was in a very small village in a grassy valley. Outside the village, cattle, sheep, goats and horses were kept in farm fields. Buti watched the cattle while his mother worked in the fields of vegetables. His sisters worked in the kitchen preparing beans, vegetables and *mealies*, a kind of corn, for dinner. It was a poor village, but Buti was a happy child. He played and fought with the other boys. In the evening he listened to his parents tell stories of long ago. They spoke of great wars with other tribes.

'Someday,' Buti told his parents, 'I will fight for my people.'

Buti's father saw that he was a clever boy, and he decided that he needed a good education. So seven-year-old Buti went to the local school. It was there that Rolihlahla 'Buti' Mandela became Nelson Mandela. The white teachers in the schools could not pronounce African names. So they gave the children new English names. Buti's teacher chose 'Nelson' for him.

Nelson did not like his new name but he liked his school. He was a good student, but his parents wanted more for Nelson. Gadla's health was not good and he worried about Nelson's future. He asked King Jongintaba to look after Nelson and make sure he continued his education. The King remembered the favour he owed to Gadla. He promised that he would give Nelson the best possible education.

When Nelson was ten, his father died. King Jongintaba sent for him. It was time for Nelson to leave Qunu. Nelson packed his little case and said goodbye to his family. He was going to Mqhekezweni, the capital of Thembuland. He was going to live with his cousin, the King.

Nelson missed his mother and sisters, but he was happy in his new home. There was much to keep him busy. He helped with the cattle and in the fields. He played with the other boys. He went to a one-room school where he studied English. He also studied the language of his tribe, and history and geography.

Nelson's teachers saw that he was an intelligent and hard-working boy. They gave him special attention.

Nelson learned to respect the King. He also had lessons in leadership and freedom of speech. At tribal meetings, all Thembus could come and speak, not just the most powerful. At the end, the King would speak and try to find agreement between everyone. If they could not agree, another meeting would take place.

The King's son, Justice, became Nelson's best friend. In 1937, when Nelson was nineteen, he went with Justice to Healdtown College, in Fort Beaufort. As always, Nelson worked hard in his studies. He made friends with Africans from other tribes. This was a new experience for Nelson. He started to feel less like a Thembu and more like an African.

Fort Hare College was a centre for students from many African countries. King Jongintaba wanted Nelson to study at Fort Hare and Nelson was happy to go there. The King bought Nelson a new suit and a pair of shiny shoes. Nelson was on his way to a new life.

At Fort Hare, Nelson discovered politics. He made many friends and enjoyed discussing political ideas with them. But Nelson's new life did not last long. He quickly saw his first chance for political action. He and his friends organized a protest to fight for students' rights. But the college did not want troublemakers in their school and Nelson and his friends were told to leave.

The King was very angry. He told Nelson to apologize[21] to the college director. But Nelson refused. There was no reason to apologize, he believed.

The King also told Nelson that it was time for him to get married. He chose a wife for Nelson and paid the usual bride price. Nelson was going to be married soon – to a stranger! Nelson respected the King and his people, but he could not agree to the marriage. So he refused the King's order. It was time for Nelson to leave Mqhekezweni.

Nelson talked to Justice and together they decided to go to the city of Johannesburg. It was the biggest, busiest city in the country. When the King heard that Nelson and Justice were in Johannesburg, he was even angrier than before. He ordered them to return. Justice returned, but Nelson asked the King to let him stay. He wanted to become a lawyer[22], he said. The King agreed. Nelson could stay in Johannesburg, he said, but he had to earn his own money.

3

The African National Congress

Mandela knew that life in Johannesburg would not be easy. He soon found a job as a policeman in a gold mine. The pay was not good, but it was enough to live on. He lived in a room in the township of Alexandria, outside Johannesburg. It was not as nice as Mqhekezweni, where he lived with the King. But Nelson did not care.

Mandela began to make new friends. One was Walter Sisulu a businessman and lawyer. Sisulu also owned an agency that helped find housing for blacks. Mandela also met some old friends too. Oliver Tambo, an old friend from college, was living and working in Johannesburg.

Mandela soon lost his job at the goldmine. He asked Walter Sisulu for advice. Sisulu knew Mandela wanted to go to law school and become a lawyer. He introduced him to a white lawyer named Lazer Sidelsky. Sidelsky's law firm was one of the biggest in the city. It had black and white clients[23]. Sidelsky was different from many of the white people of the time. He did not agree with apartheid.

Sidelsky liked Mandela, so he gave him a job as a clerk[24]. He was a kind and generous man. He gave Mandela advice and taught him about the law.

Mandela was getting used to life in the city. He had friends, a place to live and a job. He was learning to look after himself. He did not need his family or royal connections. People respected him for his intelligence, confidence[25] and warm personality. He was a serious man, but he always had a smile on his face.

Before Mandela could go to law school, he needed to finish his bachelor's degree. The University of South Africa offered

Nelson Mandela as a young law student

distance learning. This meant that Mandela could post his essays to the university.

He finished his degree in this way. Then in 1943, he began studying law at the University of the Witwatersrand. At the university he joined the International Club and learnt about Mahatma Gandhi. Gandhi was an Indian leader who was using non-violent[26] protest. He was trying to change unfair laws in India. Mandela liked what he heard about Gandhi. He wondered if peaceful protest might work in South Africa.

Mandela and his friends hoped that a better day was coming. They wanted all people in South Africa to be free and equal. But things would not get better. Soon, they would get much worse.

Mandela continued working for Lazer Sidelsky while he studied law. In his free time he often met with friends at Walter Sisulu's home. There was always talk, laughter and new people to meet. One day Walter's cousin, Evelyn, came to visit. She knew many of Walter's friends, but there was something very special about Nelson. He was interesting to talk to, and he enjoyed a good joke. Evelyn liked that, but she also liked his seriousness and his ideas. Mandela was interested in Evelyn as well. Soon they decided to get married. Their first son, Thembi, was born in 1945.

Nelson and Evelyn needed a larger place to live, so the Government gave them a house. It was a small, two-room house on a dirt road. It had a metal roof, a concrete floor and a bucket for a toilet. Soon the small house would be very crowded. First Mandela's sister, Leabie, came to live with them. Then Mandela's mother, Nosekeni Fanny, followed. Mandela was a happy man. He had a good job, a family and now he had his own home.

Mandela joined the African National Congress in 1944. Many believed that the ANC was not as strong as it had been in the 1930s. They thought there was too much talk and too

14

little action. Many young ANC members thought that it was time to fight harder for equality. Mandela agreed. In 1944, a group of about sixty ANC leaders, including Mandela, Walter Sisulu and Oliver Tambo, created the ANC Youth League.

Members of the group argued about the relationship they wanted with South Africa's white people. Some Youth League members believed that all white people should leave Africa. Africa was the blacks' homeland. These Youth League members believed they should 'run the white man into the sea'.

Mandela did not agree. He knew it was not possible for all white people to leave South Africa. More importantly, he did not believe that all white people were bad. It was the racist[27] beliefs of some white people that the ANC needed to fight. Mandela believed in a South Africa free of racism. He wanted a country where blacks, whites and other races could live together in peace. He believed that the ANC should try to make the white government change their racist laws. They must give equal rights to all non-whites in the country.

The new ANC Youth League excited many young blacks in South Africa. As the 1940s passed, membership grew and the ANC became stronger. Mandela was elected the secretary of the Youth League in 1947. As the ANC became larger and more powerful, conditions[28] for blacks in South Africa became worse. South Africa's economy[29] was growing. But as whites became richer, blacks became poorer. Hundreds of thousands of blacks had to live in the townships outside the country's cities. The conditions in the townships were terrible. Unemployment, disease and problems with the police were part of normal life. And as their lives became worse, the blacks became angrier.

At the same time, many whites in South Africa were becoming worried. In 1947, the United Nations spoke out against apartheid. Some whites felt that it was time to end the system. Many others were afraid that their lives would change

15

A black township which is now part of Soweto, 1951

for ever. They did not want the non-white majority to have control.

In 1948, there was a surprise in South African politics. The conservative National Party was elected. A group called the *Afrikaner Broederbond* helped the National Party to victory. The Broederbond was a secret group. They wanted to keep Afrikaner culture and take control of the South African Government. It was the first time that South Africa was ruled by a party which was completely Afrikaner. In his victory speech the new prime minister, Daniel Malan said, 'South Africa belongs to us once more'.

Before the election of the National Party, blacks had little freedom. Now their lives became much worse. Apartheid laws became stronger. By 1948, there were more than three thousand laws controlling blacks and other non-whites. Apartheid laws divided South Africans into four racial groups: white, black,

A 'blacks-only' bus in Johannesburg, 1984

Asian (mostly Indians) and mixed-race. Laws decided where each group could live. Laws decided where each group could travel. People were not allowed to marry people from other racial groups. Life for blacks and other non-whites in South Africa was becoming impossible.

4

Action!

After the election of the National Party, the ANC knew it was time for action. The ANC still believed in peaceful methods[30], but which methods would work best? At the ANC's yearly conference in 1949, the organisation created the Programme of Action. There would be strikes[31], protests and other kinds of non-violent action. This was an important change for the ANC. In the past, the ANC always obeyed the law. But the methods described in the new Programme of Action were illegal.

The Programme of Action caused a lot of arguments within the ANC leadership. Gandhi's peaceful mass actions in India were working. Mandela, Tambo, Sisulu and other Youth League leaders wanted to use the same methods in South Africa. But Dr AB Xuma, the president of the ANC, did not agree. He said it was too early for such actions. The Government, he said, would try to destroy[32] the ANC.

But the Youth League leaders decided to take that chance. They told Xuma to support their Programme of Action. If he did not, they would not support him in the next election for presidency. Xuma and the Youth League could not agree. So in the next election, Dr JS Moroka was elected as the new ANC president. Moroka supported the Programme of Action.

The Youth League leaders were gaining more power within the ANC. Mandela had caused this change, but there was one thing that troubled him. Many people in the ANC wanted to work with communist[33] and Indian organisations. Mandela thought this was a mistake.

The Youth League planned a Day of Protest. On this day, blacks across the country would strike – they would not go to their jobs or open their businesses. The ANC planned to affect two important trades. The economy of South Africa depended on the gold and diamond trade. The gold and diamond trade depended on black workers. If black workers refused to work in the gold and diamond mines, the mines would have to close. This would hurt the economy. It would also be a hard lesson for the Government.

Before the ANC announced the strike, the Communist Party and the South African Indian Congress also decided to protest. The date for 'Freedom Day' was set as the 1st of May 1950.

Across South Africa, thousands of blacks took part in Freedom Day. The protest was peaceful, but the police still used violence. Eighteen people were killed and many more were badly wounded[34].

After Freedom Day, the Government made it a crime[35] to be a member of the Communist Party. It was even a crime to be a communist. Mandela and Oliver Tambo understood the importance of this. If the Government could ban[36] one political party, it could ban another.

'Today it is the Communist Party,' Tambo said. 'Tomorrow it will be the ANC.'

The ANC continued making plans for their Day of Protest. It took place on the 26th of June 1950. Thousands of black businesses did not open. There was no violence. The Day of Protest was the first time the ANC tried political action. It gave them experience and confidence, but it was just the beginning.

After the Day of Protest, the Prime Minister Daniel Malan created more apartheid laws. After these laws were passed in 1951, the ANC Youth League sent a letter to the Prime Minister. The letter asked for six apartheid laws to be cancelled. If they were not, the ANC would begin a countrywide movement. They would not obey the laws.

No laws were changed and the Government gave a warning

Day of Protest, 26th June, 1950

to the ANC. They said that the police would punish anyone who disobeyed the laws.

So Mandela and the ANC began organising the Defiance Campaign[37]. The campaign asked thousands of blacks across the country to stay out after the usual night curfew. The curfew was the time when everyone must be in their homes. The campaign also told blacks to enter white-only areas, to use white-only toilets, waiting rooms, post office entrances and railway cars. This would be followed by strikes across the country.

Mandela organised the Defiance Campaign. He travelled to all parts of South Africa. This was not easy. Blacks could not stay in most hotels, and taxis would not stop to pick them up. Often Mandela had to walk from town to town. Wherever he went, Mandela spoke to large and small groups. He told them that they must work together to make a difference.

But Mandela also warned that they must not give the Government any reason to use violence. The protests had to be controlled and organised, and peaceful. Peaceful mass protests could work, he told the crowds. They were working in India and they could do the same in South Africa. Mandela was a strong speaker. The non-whites listened to his words, and they believed that change was possible. They knew it would not be easy, but they believed that they had to try.

The Defiance Campaign began on the 26th of June 1952. More than eight thousand five hundred people took part. For five months, doctors, lawyers, teachers, students, ministers and other people from all races broke the apartheid laws. The punishment was usually a small fine – they had to pay some money to the Government – and a short time in prison. The apartheid laws were not cancelled because of the Defiance Campaign, but the ANC grew stronger. ANC membership grew from twenty thousand to over one hundred thousand people. People around the world began to notice the ANC and their fight for freedom. Mandela hoped that the Government would take them seriously and talk to them.

The Government did take the ANC seriously, but they were not interested in talking.

5

Banned

The Government wanted to stop the Defiance Campaign. They also passed more laws to control the freedom of non-whites. Meetings between non-whites were banned and it became even more difficult for them to travel.

About one month after the beginning of the campaign, the police went to Mandela's house. He and his family were sleeping. The police broke down the door and took Mandela to prison. The same happened at the homes of more than twenty other ANC leaders.

The arrests[38] of the ANC leaders did not stop the campaign. But when violent mass protests began, the campaign ended. During the trouble, twelve people, black and white, were shot by the police. Many more were wounded.

The Defiance Campaign was successful in some ways. It brought the South African government's apartheid laws to the world's media. It gave the black, mixed-race and Asian people of South Africa some hope. The ANC's membership grew, and it gave the organisation experience for the fight ahead. But it did not improve the lives of South Africa's non-whites. None of the apartheid laws were cancelled.

Mandela later said that the Defiance Campaign gave him confidence. It also gave him belief that the ANC could win. The Campaign, he said, made him feel like a true 'freedom fighter'.

Mandela and the other ANC leaders were soon freed from prison. But now they were in another kind of prison – a prison without walls. Nelson Mandela and the other top leaders of the ANC were banned from:

- having meetings
- entering schools and universities
- entering airports
- entering newspaper offices
- speaking to newspapers
- speaking on the radio
- writing for newspapers or magazines
- travelling outside their township
- belonging to any organisation.

Before Mandela was banned from belonging to an organisation, he was made president of the Transvaal section of the ANC. Now that he was banned, he could not travel to the Transvaal to give his presidential speech. Another man had to read it for him. One day, Mandela's speech promised, all the people of South Africa would be free and equal. But, he warned, it would be 'no easy walk to freedom'.

Mandela now thought of himself as a freedom fighter. But even freedom fighters have to earn money. After finishing law school in 1952, Mandela worked for a few months at a white law firm. While there he would often visit his friend Oliver Tambo, who worked at another law firm nearby. The two men would talk about ANC business.

Mandela soon opened his own law firm and asked Tambo to join him. Their firm was in the centre of Johannesburg near the central court building. They were not the only black lawyers in South Africa, but Mandela and Tambo ran the only black law firm.

It was very difficult for blacks in South Africa to follow the many laws. Walking through a whites-only door was a crime. So was:

- riding on a whites-only bus
- using a whites-only drinking fountain
- walking on a whites-only beach

- being on the street after 11 p.m
- not having a pass book
- having no job
- living in the wrong place
- having no place to live.

Every morning, there was a line of blacks outside the offices of Mandela and Tambo. They were waiting for legal help. They knew that Mandela and Tambo was a place where they could talk to people of their own colour.

Oliver Tambo and Nelson Mandela in Addis Ababa, Ethiopia, 1962

Soon Mandela would again have legal problems of his own. Four miles from the centre of Johannesburg was the black township of Sophiatown. Whites in the neighbouring areas wanted to live in Sophiatown's nice houses. Also, the Government found it difficult to control blacks living inside the city. The Government decided that the non-whites of Sophiatown had to move. They had to go and live in another black township several miles outside Johannesburg.

The ANC fought the decision. One Sunday evening, Mandela spoke to a meeting in Freedom Square, in the centre of Sophiatown. The crowd was angry and Mandela felt their anger. He said that the time for peaceful action was over. Non-violence was not working, he said.

Mandela told the crowd that peaceful action would not work. They had to use violence to destroy apartheid. Young people in the crowd were cheering. They were very excited by Mandela's strong language. The policemen watching the meeting were also interested in Mandela's words. They also listened carefully and they wrote down everything that Mandela said.

In September of 1953, Mandela's ban was lifted and he was allowed to travel outside Johannesburg. He decided to travel to the small village of Villiers in the Orange Free State. When he arrived, he had an unhappy surprise. A group of policemen were waiting for him. They gave him a piece of paper which charged him with being a communist. And again he was banned, this time for two years. He was told to leave the ANC. He could not travel outside Johannesburg and could not go to any meetings.

Mandela was very upset. After ten years with the ANC, the fight for freedom 'had become my life,' he later said. He could never leave the ANC or leave the fight. Now he would have to continue his ANC work in secret.

During 1954 and 1955, the ANC continued to fight the

Government's plans for Sophiatown. But at a meeting on the 8th of February 1955, Mandela and the other ANC leaders told the people not to fight the move. They felt that using violence would be a terrible mistake.

The next day, four thousand police and soldiers began destroying the houses in Sophiatown. The ANC were not able to stop it. Mandela now believed that only armed[39] and violent action would bring change to South Africa.

6

The Freedom Charter and the Treason[40] Trial

The National Party was re-elected in 1953. They made even harder laws. One of them, the Bantu Education Act, controlled black education. In the past, most schools for blacks were run by religious people called missionaries. Now these missionary schools would be closed. All schools would be controlled directly by the Government. This way the Government knew that young blacks were not being taught about freedom and equality. The new law made people angry all over South Africa.

At first, blacks did not let their children go to the new schools. Slowly, however, blacks decided that bad schools were better than no schools. Once again, the ANC were not able to stop another government action. But the new schools did not work. The children who went to them grew up even angrier than their parents.

In the same year, the ANC had a new idea. Working with other groups, they planned a Congress of the People. They wanted to create a list of rights called a 'Freedom Charter'. The ANC and other groups could use the Freedom Charter to work together for a new South Africa.

The ANC asked more than two hundred organisations to send people to a planning conference in March 1954. At the conference, the groups decided they would collect ideas from their members. They were asked questions like, 'If you could make the laws, what would you do?' and 'How would you make South Africa a happy place to be?'

Many of the answers were collected in secret meetings.

Mandela was very busy planning the Congress, but much of his work was done in secret.

Answers began to come in. They came from sport clubs, cultural clubs, church groups, schools, work unions and women's organisations. Some spoke of the need for better pay, better education, housing and food. Others spoke of freedom and equality. But what people most wanted was fair voting rights for all – one person, one vote.

The Congress took place on the 25th and 26th of June 1955. On that day, more than three thousand people marched[41] towards a football field in the town of Kliptown, near Johannesburg. The people laughed and sang as they walked. They knew they were making history. Each, in his or her small way, was fighting for freedom.

The police stood along the road watching them. They took photos and wrote notes, but they could not do anything else. Most of the people were black. But there were hundreds of Asians, mixed race and even about a hundred white people. There were doctors, lawyers, teachers, students, housewives, ministers and farmers. They walked together carrying signs asking for freedom and equality. The black, yellow and green colours of the ANC were everywhere.

Mandela was there too. He was still banned, but he came and watched from a distance.

On the first day, the charter was read aloud.

We, the people of South Africa, want our country and the world to know:

- *that South Africa belongs to all who live in it – black and white. Its government must be voted in by the people;*
- *that land, freedom and peace were stolen from its people;*
- *that our country will never be rich until all our people can live together with equal rights and opportunities.*

The Government were asked to the conference, but instead they sent the police. On the second day of the conference, the police came with tanks[42] and guns. They said that the Congress was breaking the law and no one was allowed to leave. They surrounded the crowd with guns. The people were calm. They loudly sang 'Nkosi Sikilel' iAfrica', or 'God Bless Africa', the ANC anthem. One by one, the people were interviewed by the police and their names were written down.

The police broke up the Congress, but the Freedom Charter was written. It would give hope during the fight ahead.

The police came to Mandela's house in the early morning of the 5th of December 1956. Mandela was woken by a loud knocking on his door. A police detective and two officers entered and began searching the house. After forty five minutes, the detective told Mandela that he was under arrest. Mandela's crime was 'High Treason', which could be punished by death.

Mandela was not the only person arrested that day. Across the country, many others were arrested for the same charge. Most of the ANC leaders were taken to Johannesburg Prison. There were one hundred and fifty six prisoners; blacks, whites, Asians and mixed race, men and women. All of them would go to court for the crime of high treason.

The treason trial began on the 19th of December 1956. The prisoners were put in a large cage[43] inside the courtroom. Someone put a sign saying DO NOT FEED on the cage. When the judge saw this, he became angry. He ordered the cage to be taken from the court and he freed the prisoners on bail[44]. As the prisoners left the courthouse, a large crowd shouted 'Nkosi Sikelel iAfrica'. The police fired their guns to break up the crowd.

The trial lasted four and a half years. The ANC leaders *and* the Freedom Charter itself were on trial. The Government said that the Freedom Charter was 'communist'. The defence said that the charter's ideas were shared by people of all races and colours. These people lived in South Africa and all around

The front page of South Africa's *The World* newspaper, June 12, 1964, during the Riviona trial

the world. If the men and women on trial were guilty[45], then most people in the world were also guilty.

The trial was very difficult for those who were not from Johannesburg. Many lost their jobs or businesses. They could not stay in hotels, so they lived in the black townships. In this way, the Government actually helped the ANC. They brought all the ANC leaders together. Because of banning orders, this was almost impossible before. Now the ANC leaders could share ideas and make plans.

The trial was written about in newspapers around the world. And from around the world came support and money. The defence lawyers presented their case well.

During the trial, Mandela spoke for a long time. He sounded very confident and his English was excellent. Because of the trial, Mandela and the ANC became known and respected around the world. Finally, in March 1961, the judge made his decision. He said that Government's case was not strong enough. The men and women were *not guilty*.

7

Nomzamo Winifred Madikizela

Mandela and Evelyn had three more children. Their son Thembi was joined by another boy, Makgatho, in 1950. They also had two daughters, both called Makazwe (or Maki) in 1947 and 1953. Evelyn wanted Mandela to give up politics and return with her to Transkei. Mandela explained that politics was his life's work. They had many arguments and were finally divorced in 1957.

Not long after this, Mandela was visiting his friend Oliver Tambo. Mandela noticed a pretty girl sitting in the office with her brother. Tambo introduced the girl to Mandela. Nomzamo Winifred Madikizela was her name, but everyone called her Winnie. The next day, Nelson called Winnie to ask for her help. He wanted her to help raise money for the Treason Trial. That was what he said to Winnie, but he really just wanted to have lunch with her.

Winnie grew up in Pondoland, the same small village as Oliver Tambo. She came from a poor family, but both her parents were teachers. They made sure that she received a good education. Like Mandela, she left home because she did not want to marry a stranger.

Winnie went to Johannesburg where she graduated from the University of Witwatersrand. After her graduation, she became the first black female social worker[46] at Baragwanath Hospital. In her job she found that medical care for blacks was much worse than for whites. The suffering[47] of the blacks in South Africa made her angry. She and Mandela both wanted to fight for change.

In March 1957, Mandela asked Winnie to marry him. He warned her that marriage to a freedom fighter would not be

Nelson Mandela marries Winnie Madikizela, 14 June, 1958

easy. He had little money, he told her. Because of the Treason Trial and the bans, he had little time for his law practice. They would have to live on her small salary as a social worker. And after the Treason Trial, he might go to prison for a long time. Even if he did not go to prison, his life would always be full of problems with the police.

Mandela wanted to be sure that Winnie understood. She did, and she was still happy to say 'yes'.

At first, Winnie's father was not happy about the marriage. He was worried that Winnie was making a mistake. So Mandela travelled to her village and met her father. He promised that he would be a good husband to Winnie.

The wedding took place on the 14th of June 1958 in Winnie's village. Then Nelson had to return to Johannesburg for the Treason Trial.

Nelson and Winnie lived in the black township of Soweto. There they were lucky to have things that few others in the black townships had – electricity, hot water and an indoor toilet. Mandela's three children with Evelyn were regular visitors. Soon Mandela had two more daughters. Zeni was born in 1959 and Zindzi was born in 1960.

Mandela was right when he warned Winnie that their life together would not be easy. Early in the morning he had to take the bus to the trial in Pretoria. He often stayed there overnight. On weekends he was busy with ANC business and planning for the trial. By the late 1950s, Mandela's career as a lawyer was just about finished. Fighting for freedom and equality was now his full-time job.

8

The Sharpeville Massacre[48]

As the years passed, the Government passed more laws to control the freedom of blacks. In 1959, they created eight new 'countries' within South Africa. These would become the 'homelands' of South Africa's blacks. The blacks would no longer be from South Africa but from one of these homelands. Although blacks made up seventy percent of the population, the new homelands were only thirteen percent of South Africa's land. There was much protest and violence against this plan. And although the ANC argued against it, the plan became reality.

Life for blacks in South Africa was becoming worse, not better. This caused argument within the ANC. Many respected the idea of non-violence, but they did not think it would ever work. Younger ANC members believed that the ANC was old-fashioned.

Robert Sobukwe was a member of the ANC Youth League. In 1959, he left the ANC and created a new organization called the Pan African Congress (PAC). He did not agree with the Freedom Charter's statement that 'South Africa belongs to all who live in it, black and white'. Sobukwe called for a 'government of the Africans by the Africans and for the Africans'. The PAC did not want white members. It did not believe that whites, Asians or mixed race people could live in the new South Africa.

The PAC's first plan was an anti-pass law campaign. The ANC were already planning a similar campaign. But the PAC wanted to show that they were leading the fight. The PAC said that their campaign would begin on the 21st of March 1960. This was ten days before the ANC would begin theirs.

It was illegal for blacks to not have their passbooks. The PAC wanted blacks to give in their passbooks at police stations, then they would be arrested. If thousands of blacks did this across the country, the prisons would be filled. If enough black workers were sent to prison, the economy would be badly hurt. Then the Government would have to cancel the pass laws.

Sobukwe did not want to use violence. He told the head of police that the anti-pass protests would be peaceful.

On the morning of the 21st, Sobukwe started the campaign. He walked into a police station in the town of Orlando. He gave them his passbook and was arrested.

As the day went on, thousands of blacks gave in their passbooks. Usually they were arrested without any trouble. The protest in Johannesburg was small.

Sharpeville, a small town thirty-five miles south of Johannesburg, held a much larger protest. Police said that there were twenty thousand protestors. Others said there were five thousand. No one is sure, but there were more protestors than police. In the morning, thousands of protestors crowded around a police station. There were only twelve police officers on duty. Two-hundred more police arrived by noon, but there were still many more protestors.

The police ordered the crowd to leave. When they did not, aeroplanes dropped tear gas[49] on the people below. The crowd were frightened and moved towards the police. Suddenly the police began shooting at the crowd.

When the shooting stopped, sixty nine people were dead. Most of the dead were shot in the back as they ran away from the police.

The Sharpeville massacre was international news. Terrible pictures on television showed police holding guns. They were standing near dead and dying blacks. The Sharpeville massacre woke the world up to apartheid in South Africa.

The other ANC leaders supported the PAC after the

The Sharpeville massacre, 21 March, 1960

massacre. On the 26th of March, the president of the ANC publicly burned his passbook. On the 28th of March, Mandela did the same. The ANC called for a Day of Mourning[50]. Hundreds of thousands of angry protestors filled the streets. Frightened whites began buying guns. Many whites left the country. The stock exchange[51] fell. The United Nations said that the South African government was responsible for the massacre.

The Government called a 'state of emergency'. Police could now arrest anyone for any reason. Twenty thousand people were arrested and the PAC and ANC were banned. Eighteen hundred of their members, including Nelson Mandela, were arrested. Robert Sobukwe, was sent to prison for three years. When the three years were finished, he was kept in prison for three more years.

The ANC was now a secret, illegal organization.

9

Spear of the Nation

In 1961, South Africa left the British Commonwealth. The South African government was angry with Queen Elizabeth because she did not agree with apartheid. A new constitution – set of rules – was going to be written. Mandela wrote a letter to the Prime Minister. He wanted the new constitution to be colour-free. The Prime Minister never replied. The Government would not talk to Mandela and they were still making blacks go to the tribal homelands.

Mandela and the other ANC leaders were now sure that non-violence was not working. In a secret meeting in June 1961, the ANC leaders made plans. They talked about the kind of violence they would use. Some of the leaders wanted to use terrorism[52] but Mandela was not happy about this. He wanted to hurt the South African economy but he did not want people to be killed. He believed that property should be attacked[53] rather than people. The other leaders agreed and made Mandela the leader of an armed section of the ANC. The section was called Umkhonto we Sizwe (Spear of the Nation). The section would attack military buildings, railways, phone lines and power stations.

Mandela was taking a dangerous road. He had to hide from the police. He could not even live in his own home. Mandela was busy finding members for the Spear. The new members were sent out of the country to learn how to explode bombs. Sometimes Mandela went out of the country too. He hid by day and travelled by night. He stayed with friends or in empty flats. Living apart from his family was difficult but there was no other way. In the town of Rivonia there was a secret farm.

There Mandela and other ANC leaders hid from the police and held meetings. Sometimes Winnie and the children were able to meet Mandela there.

The Spear first attacked in December 1961. Bombs exploded at power stations and government offices in three cities. The Government were shocked. White South Africans were shocked too. Now, said Mandela, they understood 'that they were sitting on top of a volcano'.

After hiding from the police for eighteen months, Mandela was caught in August 1962. He was found guilty of leaving the country. The punishment was five years in prison with hard labour[54].

In the summer of 1963, Walter Sisulu and eight other ANC leaders were arrested at the farm in Rivonia. The police also took away maps, letters and other papers. These papers showed them that Mandela was involved[55] with the Spear of the Nation. In October 1963, the Rivonia Trial began. Again, Mandela was on trial. He was charged with attacking buildings and planning protests. The punishment could be death.

Mandela knew that newspapers around the world would be writing about the trial. He decided not to defend himself. Instead, he would use the trial to show the world about apartheid. He would put the Government on trial.

It took the Government five months to present its case against Mandela. When its lawyers had finished, Mandela did not defend himself. He did, however, make a statement. It lasted four hours. His statement spoke of the terrible suffering and unfairness that was everyday life for blacks in South Africa.

On the 11th of June 1963 the judge made his decision. He found Mandela guilty and sentenced him to life in prison.

10

Robben Island

Mandela was sent to Robben Island, a small island twelve kilometres from the coast of Cape Town. Escape from Robben Island was impossible.

Mandela could not even speak to the other prisoners. He was put in a section of the prison where he could not talk to anyone. Mandela's world was now a two metre by two metre cell with one small light, a mat and two blankets for sleeping. There was no water and no toilet, only a bucket that was emptied daily.

Mandela had almost no contact with the outside world. He was allowed only two letters a year. The letters could not be more than five hundred words long and could not discuss politics. They could only discuss family and personal matters. For Mandela, the worst part of being in prison was being separated from his family. Winnie and the children were more than one thousand six hundred kilometres away. Children between the ages of two and sixteen were not allowed to visit. When he went to prison, his daughter Zindzi was two and Zeni was three. Mandela did not see Zeni again for twenty years.

Mandela was only allowed visitors twice a year, and the visits were only thirty minutes long. To see her husband, Winnie had to write for permission. Then she had to let the police know when she would leave and how she would travel to Robben Island. Then she had to tell them when she would return. When she arrived at the prison, she had to sign a piece of paper. The paper promised that she would not talk about politics, prison conditions or the outside world. When she was finally able to speak to Mandela, it was through a thick glass window.

Prisoners breaking limestone at Robben Island prison

Sometimes Mandela and the other prisoners collected seaweed from the beach, but most days were spent working in the limestone quarry[56]. They used shovels and hammers[57] to break the limestone apart. In the summer the bright sun reflected off the limestone and hurt the eyes of the prisoners. In the winter they worked in the cold rain. They returned to their cells with aching backs, cut hands and covered with dirt.

Mandela decided that he would not let prison destroy him. He felt sure that someday he would be freed and he and his people would be free. He hoped and planned for a brighter future. He exercised in the morning and studied at night. He even studied the Afrikaner culture and the Afrikaans language. When the guards were not watching, he and the other prisoners talked and made plans. He was always happy and friendly to the prison guards. Many of the guards respected and liked him. Sometimes they helped him in small ways. They brought him food and gave him newspapers.

Mandela and the other prisoners got news of the outside world from new prisoners. They would talk while working in the quarry.

The younger prisoners respected Mandela. To them, he was a famous freedom fighter. He spoke for them and helped them with their problems. He organised hunger strikes and work slow downs until prison conditions got better. Little by little, there were small improvements. The prisoners were given small desks, blankets, hot water and better food. More visits and letters were allowed.

But there were dark days for Mandela. In 1969, he was called to the prison's main office. He was handed a letter from his youngest son, Makgatho. It said that Thembi, Mandela's oldest son, was dead. He was killed in a motor accident. Mandela was not allowed to go to the funeral[58].

Mandela missed Winnie, but he was proud that she was still fighting against apartheid. In 1969, Winnie was arrested and charged with secretly working with the ANC. She spent seventeen months in prison. In the years that followed, her situation became worse. She was often banned, arrested and sent to prison. In 1977, she had to move to a small house in the country without heat or electricity. She was put under house arrest. This meant that she could not leave the house in the evenings or weekends and she could not see her family or friends. It was impossible to visit her husband in prison. Her house was set on fire.

In the years that followed, Winnie Mandela became a respected leader in the fight.

The change in Winnie showed the change in the times. The Government thought that putting Mandela and other leaders in prison would stop the fight for freedom. They were very wrong. A storm was coming.

11

The Fight Continues

By banning organisations and putting their leaders in prison, the South African government had controlled a generation[59] of freedom fighters. But a younger generation was growing up. After a quiet period in the nineteen sixties, black anger was rising again in the nineteen seventies. Younger leaders were ready to fight apartheid.

One of these new leaders was Steve Biko. In 1968, Steve Biko created the South African Students' Organisation (SASO) and became their first president. Biko was a strong speaker and writer. Blacks, he said, felt sad and angry because of the terrible way they were treated. Blacks needed to be proud of their colour and proud of their culture.

Biko and his organisation created clinics in poor black areas. They also started reading and writing programmes and skills training programmes. As Biko and his ideas became more popular, the Government became more worried. In 1973, Biko was banned from leaving his hometown. He could not speak in public, and no one could visit him. The police watched and troubled him constantly.

Biko founded SASO at the age of only twenty two. At the age of twenty six, he was banned. At the age of thirty one, he was dead. He was arrested for the fourth time on the 18th of August 1977. In prison three weeks later, he was beaten to death by police. Twenty thousand people went to his funeral. They included government representatives from Great Britain, the United States, Germany and France. Biko had been against violence. His violent death shocked and angered the world.

Soweto was the name of a huge black township outside Johannesburg. More than half a million mostly poor blacks

Crowds in London remember Stephen Biko, 1997

lived there. The buildings were in a very bad condition. The streets were filled with rubbish. The blacks in Soweto were angry about apartheid laws, the lack of good jobs and good housing. But there was nothing new about that. Life for most people was unhappy, but it was also peaceful.

But in June 1976, Soweto exploded. What caused the explosion was a new government policy. The Government decided that most education had to be in Afrikaans. Most teachers and most black students could not speak Afrikaans. English was the language of Britain, the USA and international communication. Afrikaans was the language of the South African government.

People were very angry about the decision. Teachers refused to teach and students refused to write their exams. On the morning of the 16th of June 1976, twenty thousand Soweto high school students protested against the new policy. The protest was not planned. There were no leaders. Some of the protesters were under ten years old.

And then the police began shooting. There was no warning. There were no orders to break up the protest. The first person to die was thirteen-year-old Hector Peterson. He was shot in the back. The police used tear gas, but the crowd continued to move toward the police. One after another, children and teenagers fell dead or wounded. Some screamed and ran. Some threw stones and bricks at the police. The situation was now out of control. Soon hundreds more police arrived. Helicopters dropped more tear gas.

The protest continued through the night. Twenty-five people died on the first day. By the next day, Soweto was a war zone. The air was filled with tear gas and smoke from burning buildings. Police and army soldiers moved around with guns. They shot at anything that moved. Government buildings, banks and shops were destroyed. The fighting spread to other townships. For three days Soweto was out of control. Hundreds – perhaps more than one thousand people – were killed. Thousands of students refused to go to their classes. Five hundred teachers left their jobs. The violence spread to

The Soweto uprising, June 1976

other parts of the country. It was fifteen months before the Government took back control.

Nelson Mandela, far away on Robben Island, did not hear about the Soweto protests for some time. When he did, his heart ached for the dead people and children. But he was happy to know that the fight for freedom was continuing.

International pressure[60] to end apartheid grew in the 1970s and 1980s. Religious leaders, politicians, popular entertainers and sports stars spoke against it. In 1974, the United Nations cancelled South Africa's membership. Soccer and rugby teams around the world refused to play against South African teams. South Africa was banned from the Olympics.

The South African economy suffered too. People in other countries stopped buying South African products. Many companies stopped trading with South African companies. In 1973, some Arab and other African countries stopped selling oil to South Africa. The country has no oil of its own, so this was a serious problem.

Many white South Africans were starting to understand that change had to come. If not, the violence, world pressure and economic suffering would only get worse. In 1978, the Prime Minister, PW Botha warned that the country must 'adapt[61] or die'.

There were small changes. Blacks were allowed to own property in the townships. They were allowed to use whites-only hotels, restaurants, taxis, parks, theatres and lifts. Some townships got electricity.

But these were only small changes. The 'new' apartheid had no affect on the serious problems of poor education, health care and unemployment. The Government still ruled that all education should be in Afrikaans. It was almost impossible for blacks to get a good education. At the same time, many companies were suffering because they did not have enough skilled workers. More and more skilled white workers were leaving South Africa. To fill the jobs of the white workers, many companies broke the apartheid rules. They offered free high school and college courses to blacks if they promised to work for the company.

The National Party, which ruled the country, felt it could not make anyone happy. Their changes were not enough. The non-whites of South Africa wanted much more but white supporters of the National Party were angry as well. For them any change was too much. The Government told the whites that they would not lose control of the country but most whites did not believe it. The country's population was thirty three million, but only five million were white. And the black population was growing much faster than the white population.

In 1984, there were violent protests in townships in several cities. Thousands were killed. Government buildings and white-owned shops were burnt. Thousands of students no longer went to any school. They marched and carried signs saying 'Freedom before education'. Now the empty school buildings were used by the army. They were bases for the soldiers who watched the townships.

South Africa was about to begin the most troubled period in its history. On the 21st of March 1985, police shot at protestors. Twenty-one people were killed, and hundreds were wounded. The police said that the protestors were throwing petrol bombs and stones at them. But no petrol bombs were found. People who saw the shootings said that the police put stones next to the dead.

Prime Minister Botha called a state of emergency in 1985. Journalists were not allowed to report the news freely and the Government told them what they could say or not say. White South Africans lived in fear of a black rebellion[62]. South Africa became the most armed country in the world. Five million whites owned thirteen million guns. Thousands of people were arrested and held in prison without trial. Sometimes they were held as long as three years. Many were wounded and killed.

The largest strike in South Africa's history happened on the 6th of June, 1988. Nearly two million blacks stayed away from their jobs for three days. Striking workers were met with violence by the police. Ten workers were killed.

Violence moved to the countryside. The number of people arrested grew every day. In the Alexandra Township, twenty three people were killed at a funeral. In the riot that followed, much of the township was burnt to the ground. Across the country, millions of blacks fought the police and soldiers. In 1961, Mandela had warned that the South African government 'were sitting on top of a volcano'. Now the volcano was exploding.

International pressure against apartheid grew stronger. Twelve European countries took their representatives out of South Africa. The Pope spoke against apartheid. In June 1986, the British government warned that there would be a 'bloodbath' if apartheid did not end soon. In the same year, the United States Congress passed economic sanctions against South Africa. Sanctions are laws which punish a country. The sanctions passed by Congress made it illegal for Americans to invest money in South Africa. Many American companies would not have any business contact with South Africa. Great Britain and other European countries also passed sanctions.

Many British, American, German and Swiss banks asked South African banks to pay back loans to their countries immediately. South Africa was now hated by the rest of the world. The economy was suffering terribly. The country's currency[63], the rand, fell to its lowest ever level on the stock exchange. The country entered its worst recession[64] in fifty years.

There was one man who might help. In the past, the Government had not been interested in talking to him. Now they were very interested. That man was Nelson Mandela.

12

Free Mandela!

More and more young prisoners came to Robben Island. Mandela taught them about the law and politics. He gave them advice that would help them to become future leaders of South Africa. Then, one evening in 1982, Mandela and Walter Sisulu were secretly moved from Robben Island to Pollsmoor Maximum Security Prison. No reason was given for the move. Mandela thought that the Government was upset because Robben Island prison was becoming 'Mandela University'. That was true, but Mandela later learned that there was another reason.

His fellow prisoners at Robben Island were his friends. He missed them, but Pollsmoor was better than Robben Island. The food was better, and there was a library and a radio.

In 1984, Mandela had a surprise. During visits, he and Winnie were no longer separated by thick glass. For the first time in twenty one years, Mandela could touch his wife.

The world had not forgotten Nelson Mandela. The opposite was true. The campaign to free him was growing in strength. Pressure from the outside world continued. Around the world there were protests. People marched in the streets shouting 'Free Mandela!' Mandela was given awards from human rights groups. Streets, schools and parks were given his name. As hate for apartheid grew, so did love for Nelson Mandela.

The South African government finally understood that Mandela was the only man who could change things. In January 1985, President Botha offered to free him. But first he said that Mandela had to stop the violence. He also had to agree to the tribal homeland policy and to live in his tribal homeland, Transkei.

Concert calling for Nelson Mandela to be freed, London, 1988

Mandela's answer was 'no', but the Government were still interested in talking to him. Later in 1985, Mandela went to hospital for a small operation. There, he had a surprise visitor, Kobie Coetsee. Coetsee was a high member of the Government and he worked closely with President Botha. Mandela and Coetsee did not talk about politics but Mandela understood that the Government were making an important move. They wanted to continue talking to him. He also understood the real reason for moving him to Pollsmoor Prison. It had made it easier for the Government to meet with him.

It was now clear that Mandela would be freed someday. It was not a question of *if* but *when*. It was a big step for the National Party to talk to black leaders. And it was not an easy step. Many white South Africans were against the idea.

After Mandela returned to prison, Coetsee continued talking in secret with him. Coetsee was also talking with

Oliver Tambo, who was living in Britain.

But then Mandela became sick again. This time it was worse. Mandela had tuberculosis, a very serious disease. People around the world were very worried about him. The Government was worried too. If Mandela died, their best hope of political change would die with him.

The Government gave Mandela the best care available, and Mandela slowly recovered. But as he got better, South Africa's problems became worse. Mandela decided to write to President Botha. He said that he would talk to the Government but, he told Botha, the ANC wanted equal voting rights for blacks. Mandela also told Botha that he understood the worries of the whites. He wanted to find a way to protect them.

Botha wanted to meet with him. People thought Botha was bad-tempered and unpleasant. Mandela was ready for this. But Mandela was surprised. Botha was friendly and respectful, and the meeting went well. There were more meetings, but in the end, nothing happened.

In 1989, Botha was replaced by a new leader, FW de Klerk. De Klerk was a big supporter of apartheid. But now the situation in South Africa was so bad that he had no choice. He saw the need for action and he took it. He began talks with Mandela and the ANC.

They were strange talks. Although Mandela was in prison, he made all the demands[65]. He would not agree to his freedom unless those demands were met. The demands were as follows:

- all political prisoners must be freed
- all non-whites must have the right to vote
- all bans on political parties must end.

De Klerk agreed to some of the demands, but not all of them. Mandela was patient. He knew it was important to wait, and not too expect too much. Finally, De Klerk and Mandela agreed on a plan.

**President FW De Klerk and Nelson Mandela speaking to
television and newspaper reporters in May 1990**

On the 2nd of February 1990, De Klerk spoke to South
Africa's government in Cape Town. People across South Africa
watched on television. De Klerk shocked the country as he
told them that the ANC and sixty other organisations would
be made legal. This meant that three hundred and seventy four
political prisoners would be freed. He also said that the state
of emergency would soon be ended. Work on a plan to give all
South Africans a vote would also begin. Finally, he said the
words that so many wanted to hear.

'Mr Nelson Mandela will be freed ...'

Mandela left prison on the 11th of February 1990. He was
forty five when he entered prison. Now he was seventy one.
After twenty seven years, Nelson Mandela was free at last.
The blacks and other non-whites of South Africa were free
at last. Across South Africa, hundreds of thousands of blacks
celebrated[66] in the streets.

Nelson Mandela speaking to 120,000 ANC supporters after being freed from prison, 13 February, 1990

Mandela was driven to Cape Town's Grand Parade. More than one hundred thousand people were waiting to see him. 'Our march to freedom is irreversible[67]', Mandela told the crowd from the balcony of the City Hall.

A few days later, one hundred and twenty thousand people came to Soweto's football stadium to see him. Nearly one hundred thousand more listened outside the stadium. Mandela, Walter Sisulu and other ANC leaders arrived in a helicopter. Mandela spoke of his sadness at the high crime rate in the townships. He told the whites that they would have a place in the new South Africa.

'… A new South Africa without apartheid will be a better home for all,' he said.

He warned the Government that the people needed more than promises. Until apartheid was really ended, the ANC were still ready to fight. 'We are going forward', he promised.

When his speech was finished, thousands of balloons rose into the sky.

Now it was time for Mandela to see his family. The helicopter rose into the sky and took him to his home. Winnie, his children and grandchildren were waiting for him.

Mandela became deputy president of the ANC. The Government, Mandela said, had to keep its promises. No talks could take place until the state of emergency was ended. All political prisoners had to be freed and the soldiers had to leave the townships.

In May, the Government and the ANC tried to answer the problem of political prisoners. To the ANC, anyone fighting apartheid was a political prisoner. But the Government believed that all murderers and terrorists should be in prison. The reasons for their crimes did not matter.

The state of emergency was ended. The law which separated all buildings and services was cancelled. This meant that there would no longer be separate entrances, separate toilets or separate drinking fountains for whites and non-whites.

These were all good decisions. But 'twenty seven years ago, I had no vote,' Mandela said. '... I still have no vote and that is due to the colour of my skin'. He told the outside world not to end sanctions until everyone had the right to vote.

Mandela's doctors were worried that he was too old and weak for so much activity. But Mandela would not rest.

He and the ANC leaders knew that talks with the Government would be slow and difficult. Many younger blacks could not understand this. They did not want to talk to the Government, they wanted to destroy it.

The world loved Nelson Mandela. In the first week of June 1990, he left South Africa for a six week trip to fourteen countries. His first stop was Paris to meet with François Mitterrand, the French president. From France he went to Switzerland, Italy and the Netherlands. Next he went to

England where he met with Oliver Tambo. From England he flew to the USA. He spent twelve days there, visiting eight cities. Wherever he went, he was welcomed as a hero. Fifty thousand people crowded the Yankee Stadium to hear him speak. In New York he spoke to the United Nations and asked them to continue the sanctions. The next week he met with President George Bush and gave a speech to Congress.

After the USA, Mandela went to Canada and Ireland. Then he went back to England where he met with Prime Minister Margaret Thatcher. The Prime Minister was worried about Mandela's health. But after twenty seven years in prison, Mandela was enjoying freedom too much to slow down.

Nelson Mandela meeting Margaret Thatcher at 10 Downing Street, 4 July, 1990

13

Last Steps

In 1953, Nelson Mandela made one of his most famous speeches. In the speech he warned that there would be 'no easy walk to freedom'. He was right. The walk to freedom was not easy. Though the end was near, the last few steps would still be filled with problems.

The following weeks and months were a time of great hope. It was also a time when many South African organisations and people disagreed. And there were worse problems. All hoped that there would be peace after Mandela was freed. But the violence got worse. Between 1990 and 1994, thirteen thousand people died from political violence.

From its earliest days, the ANC wanted a single government which was not white or black. This also meant that tribal politics would not be part of the Government. The differences[68] between South Africa's many tribes were becoming a big problem. Mandela and the ANC wanted the people to think of themselves as South African. They must not think of themselves as white, black, mixed race, Asian, Thembu, Zulu or Xhosa.

This ANC policy was not popular. The National Party and many black organisations and tribes fought against it. This was a problem for Mandela. His biggest problem was with the Inkatha Freedom Party (IFP). Most of the members were Zulus. Zulus in South Africa have always been proud and independent. They did not want to become lost in the new government.

Several times in 1990, IFP members attacked and killed ANC members. Mandela saw that the attacks were worse when the police were involved. Mandela began to think that de Klerk was involved in the violence. When there was trouble between ANC and IFP supporters, the police always supported the IFP. They would join the IFP to attack the ANC. Perhaps, Mandela thought, de Klerk wanted blacks to fight each other. Then they would not be strong against the National Party.

In January 1991, Mandela and the IFP leader worked out an agreement to end the violence. But it did not end.

In April, Mandela told de Klerk to take control of the police and soldiers who were attacking the ANC. Finally, in May 1991, Mandela sent an angry letter to de Klerk. He said that the ANC would stop all talks if the violence did not stop. One week later, the ANC stopped the talks.

Three weeks later, the Government finally cancelled several laws controlling where blacks could live. They also started to control the actions of the police. Living conditions for blacks began to improve. Many blacks saw that Nelson Mandela was their best hope for a better and more peaceful future.

The first ANC conference inside South Africa for over thirty years took place in July 1991. There Nelson Mandela was made president of the ANC.

By this time Mandela also had serious personal problems. In April 1992, he told the ANC that he and Winnie were separating. In the twenty seven years that Mandela was in prison, their lives had gone in different directions. In the 1980s Winnie shocked many people with her angry language. In 1991, she went to prison for planning the murder of a fourteen-year-old police informer[69].

In May 1992, the real work of creating a new constitution and planning an election began. It was a long and difficult process. As usual, every group had a different idea. Black organisations did not want to work with each other. The National Party did not want to give up power.

And there was more violence. In June, a group of armed IFP members killed forty six ANC members. Mandela called

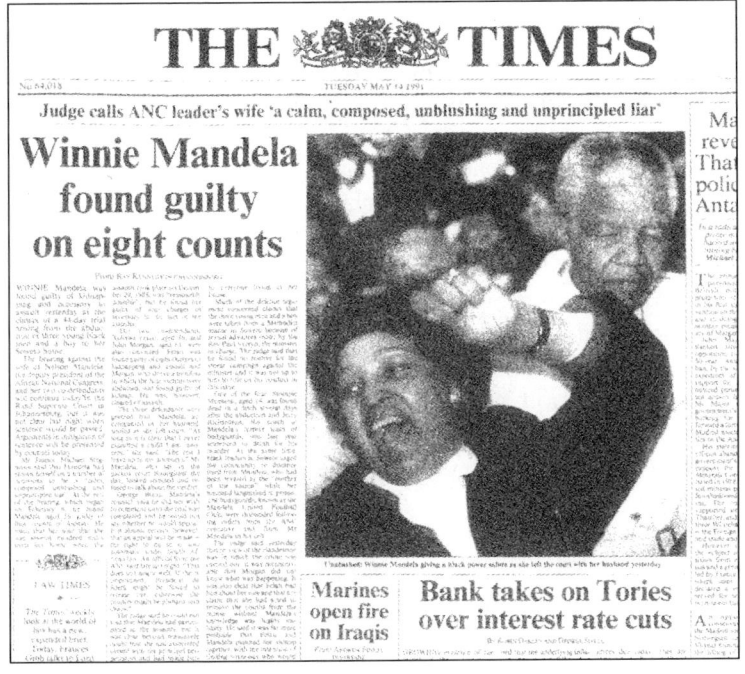

The Times front page, 10 May, 1994

for a nationwide strike. On the 3rd and 4th of August, four million workers stayed at home. It was the largest strike in South African history.

In September, government soldiers killed twenty nine people and wounded two hundred more at an ANC meeting.

But slowly the level of violence lessened. In April 1993, twenty six political and tribal groups agreed on a date for a general election. That date was the 27th of April 1994. To no one's surprise, the ANC's candidate[70] for the presidency of South Africa was Nelson Mandela.

In December, Mandela and de Klerk were awarded the Nobel Peace Prize[71].

Campaigning for the election began in February. Mandela and the other ANC candidates travelled all over the country. They met with people in towns and in villages. They listened to their hopes, fears, ideas and complaints. The ANC did not expect people to vote for them simply because they had fought apartheid for eighty years. They wanted to people to vote for them because they had the best plan for South Africa.

Mandela told blacks that they must have patience. Change, he said, would not come immediately. He told whites that South Africa was their land too. He did not want them to leave the country. '…we should forget the past and try to build a better future for all,' he said.

As the election got closer, violence grew. Around the country hundreds were killed in fighting between political groups or by the police. As usual, the IFP was at the centre of the violence. On the 28th of March, thousands of IFP members attacked the ANC headquarters in Johannesburg. Fifty three people were killed.

Finally, election day came.

14

The Whole World Watches

On the 27th of April 1994, the whole world was watching South Africa. Millions of people waited in line for hours to vote. Some old and sick people had to be carried to the voting places. Officials from other countries were there watching. They wanted to make sure the elections were fair.

It would take many days to count the votes but it was soon clear who the winner was. The new president was a man who had done more for the people of South Africa than anyone else. The new president was a man who believed that people of all races and colours could live together in peace and equality. The new president was Nelson Mandela.

Nelson Mandela was made South Africa's president on the 10th of May 1994. It was the largest ever gathering of international leaders in South Africa. FW de Klerk was made deputy president. The hard work of building a new country could begin.

Mandela's term in office was a time of great challenges and great progress. South Africa was really two countries. He had to get all South Africans to think of themselves as one people. And he had to share out government services equally.

Now that apartheid was ended, economic sanctions were lifted. This brought much needed trade, which helped the economy.

Mandela did what he thought was right. He did not do what the US wanted him to do. He had friendly relations with Palestinian leader Yasser Arafat and Libya's Muammar Gaddafi. He also helped two countries to reach peace agreements – Burundi and the Democratic Republic of Congo.

In 1996, Mandela began a relationship with Graça Machel, the widow[72] of Mozambique's former president. She became Mandela's third wife on his eightieth birthday in 1998.

The work on completing a new constitution continued during Mandela's term in office. In December 1996, Mandela signed the constitution. It created a government based on majority rule. It also protected freedom of speech for all.

Mandela resigned[73] as ANC president in 1997. He resigned the South African presidency in 1999.

In 2004, at the age of eighty five, Nelson Mandela retired[74]. He had spent his life fighting for freedom and equality. It had been a long and difficult journey, but he had won. He also had the love and respect of millions. Now it was time to rest.

Nelson Mandela in Pretoria during his inauguration as President of South Africa, 10 May, 1994

Points for Understanding

1

1 Which country did the Boers come from?
2 Why was the African National Congress created?
3 What was *apartheid*?

2

1 Why was Rolihlahla's father important?
2 What did Rolihlahla's name mean?
3 What happened after Nelson's father died?
4 What did Nelson do after the King chose a wife for him?

3

1 Who was Walter Sisulu?
2 Why was Nelson interested in Mahatma Gandhi?
3 Why was the ANC Youth League created?
4 How did Nelson Mandela disagree with other ANC Youth League leaders?

4

1 How was the Programme of Action an important change for the ANC?
2 What was the Defiance Campaign?

5

1 How did the Government try to stop the Defiance Campaign?
2 Was the Defiance Campaign successful, unsuccessful or both? Explain your answer.

6

1 How did the Bantu Education Act change education for black children?
2 Why did the ANC want a Congress of the People?
3 What happened to Mandela after the Congress of the People?
4 What was the result of the Treason Trial?

7

1 Why did Mandela invite Nomzamo Winifred 'Winnie' Madikizela to lunch?
2 What did Mandela warn Winnie about before they were married?
3 What did Mandela promise to Winnie's father? Why?

8

1 What were 'tribal homelands'?
2 What did many younger ANC members think about the policy of non-violence?
3 What happened at Sharpeville in 1960?

9

1 What methods did the Spear of the Nation use?
2 What was the result of the Rivonia Trial?

10

1 What was Robben Island?
2 Describe Mandela's life on Robben Island.
3 What is meant by: *Mandela decided that he would not let prison destroy him.*

11

1 Who was Steve Biko?
2 What happened at Soweto in 1976?
3 What are 'sanctions'?
4 Why did the Government change its mind about talking to
  Nelson Mandela?

12

1 Why was Robben Island called 'Mandela University'?
2 Did the world forget Nelson Mandela? Explain your answer.
3 What did Prime Minister Botha offer Mandela in 1985?
4 What was Mandela's answer to Botha's offer?
5 When Mandela made an offer to De Klerk, what did he
  demand?

13

1 Did the violence end after Mandela was freed from prison?
  Explain your answer.
2 Why was the Inkatha Freedom Party against the ANC's plan
  for a non-tribal government?
3 What important award was given to Mandela and de Klerk in
  December 1993?

14

1 What was special about the election in April 1994?
2 In what way was South Africa 'two countries'?
3 What were some of the most important events of Mandela's
  term in office?

Glossary

1 **ruler** (page 5)
   someone who controls a country.
2 **ancestor** (page 5)
   someone who lived a long time ago and is related to you.
3 **majority** – *the black majority* (page 5)
   the *majority* is most of the people or things in a group. There were
   more black people than white people in South Africa, but the
   white people were the rulers.
4 **trading post** (page 5)
   a small town, village, or shop far away from other towns. *Trading* is
   the activity of buying and selling goods.
5 **refused** – *to refuse* (page 5)
   to say that you will not do or accept something, or will not let
   someone do something.
6 **slave** (page 5)
   someone who belongs by law to another person and who has to
   obey them and work for them.
7 **weapon** (page 5)
   an object that can be used for hurting people or damaging property,
   for example a gun, knife, or bomb.
8 **illegal** (page 5)
   not allowed by the law.
9 **equal rights** (page 5)
   a right is something that you are morally or legally allowed to do or
   have. If you have *equal rights* you are allowed to do or have the same
   things as other people. The British changed the law so that black
   people had the same rights as white people.
10 **tribe** (page 6)
   a large group of related families who live in the same area and have
   the same language, religion, and customs.
11 **spears and clubs** (page 6)
   a *spear* is a long weapon that is like a stick with one sharp pointed
   end. A *club* is a thick heavy stick used as a weapon. The black tribes
   did not have guns.
12 **the British Empire** (page 7)
   the countries of the world ruled by Britain between the 17th
   century and the middle of the 20th century.

13 **created** – *to create* (page 7)
to make something new exist or happen.
14 **mine** (page 7)
a tunnel in the ground from which people take coal, gold, etc.
15 **system** (page 7)
a way of organizing things or doing things.
16 **respected** (page 8)
admired and approved of by many people.
17 **chief** (page 8)
the leader of a tribe.
18 **adviser** (page 8)
someone whose job is to give advice on subjects.
19 **obey** – *to obey* (page 8)
to do what a person, law, or rule says that you must do.
20 **magistrate** (page 8)
a judge in a court for minor crimes.
21 **apologize** – *to apologize* (page 11)
to tell someone that you are sorry for doing something wrong.
22 **lawyer** (page 11)
someone whose profession is to provide people with legal advice
and services.
23 **client** (page 12)
someone who uses the services of a professional person such as a
lawyer, or of a business or organization that provides help or advice.
24 **clerk** (page 12)
someone whose job is to look after the documents in an office.
25 **confidence** (page 12)
the belief that you are able to do things well.
26 **non-violent** (page 14)
something that is *violent* uses physical force to hurt people or
damage property. *Non-violent* protest uses peaceful methods to
achieve political change.
27 **racist** (page 15)
a *race* is a group of people who are similar because they have the
same skin colour or other physical features. *Racism* is a way of
behaving or thinking that shows that you believe your race is better
than others. Behaviour or thinking of this kind is described as *racist*.
28 **conditions** (page 15)
the situation or environment in which something happens or
someone lives.

29 **economy** (page 15)
the system by which a country's trade, industry, and money are organized, and all the business, industry, and trade in that system.

30 **method** (page 18)
a way of doing something, especially a planned or established way.

31 **strike** (page 18)
a period of time when people refuse to work, as a protest.

32 **destroy** – *to destroy* (page 18)
to damage or harm something so much that it cannot exist as it was before.

33 **communist** (page 18)
involving people who support *communism* – a political and economic system in which people cannot own property or industries and all groups of society are treated equally.

34 **wounded** – *to wound someone* (page 19)
to injure someone so that their body is seriously damaged.

35 **crime** (page 9)
an activity or action that is not allowed by the law.

36 **ban** (page 9)
to say officially that something is illegal or not allowed.

37 **campaign** (page 20)
a series of actions that are intended to achieve something such as social or political change.

38 **arrest** (page 22)
a situation in which the police take a person to a police station because they think that he or she has committed a crime.

39 **armed** (page 26)
carrying a weapon, or involving the use of weapons.

40 **treason** (page 27)
the crime of trying to harm or destroy your country's government.

41 **marched** – *to march* (page 28)
to walk to a place as part of an organized group which is protesting about something.

42 **tank** (page 29)
a very strong military vehicle with a large gun on the top.

43 **cage** (page 29)
a container that is made of wire or metal bars, used for keeping birds or animals in.

44 **bail** (page 29)
money that is given to a court so that someone is allowed to stay out of prison until their trial.

45 **guilty** (page 29)
   someone who is guilty has committed a crime or has done something wrong.
46 **social worker** (page 32)
   someone who is trained to give help and advice to people who have serious social problems.
47 **suffering** (page 32)
   mental or physical pain or problems.
48 **massacre** (page 35)
   the action of killing a lot of people.
49 **tear gas** (page 36)
   a gas that makes your eyes sting. It is used by the police for controlling crowds.
50 **mourning** (page 37)
   expressions of sadness because someone has died.
51 **stock exchange** (page 37)
   a place where people buy and sell shares in companies.
52 **terrorism** (page 38)
   the use of violence in order to achieve political aims.
53 **attacked** – *to attack* (page 38)
   to use violence against a person or place.
54 **hard labour** (page 39)
   very difficult physical work that some people have to do when they are in prison.
55 **involved** – *to involve* (page 39)
   someone who is involved in something takes part in it.
56 **quarry** (page 41)
   a place where stone is dug up out of the ground.
57 **shovels and hammers** (page 41)
   a *shovel* is a tool that is used for lifting and moving something such as snow or soil. It consists of a long handle with a curved metal end. A *hammer* is a tool used for hitting nails into wood. It consists of a handle and a heavy metal top.
58 **funeral** (page 42)
   a ceremony that takes place after someone dies, and the formal process of taking the body to the place where it is buried.
59 **generation** (page 43)
   all the people, a group of people, or the members of a family who are born and live around the same time.
60 **pressure** (page 46)
   attempts to persuade or force someone to do something.

61 **adapt** (page 47)

to change your ideas or behaviour to deal with a new situation.

62 **rebellion** (page 48)

an attempt to remove a government or leader by force.

63 **currency** (page 49)

the money that is used in a particular country.

64 **recession** (page 49)

a period when the economy is not successful and there is a lot of unemployment.

65 **demand** (page 52)

a firm statement that you want something.

66 **celebrated** – *to celebrate* (page 53)

to do something enjoyable in order to show that an occasion or event is special.

67 **irreversible** (page 54)

impossible to change or bring back to a previous condition or situation.

68 **differences** (page 57)

disagreements about something.

69 **informer** (page 58)

someone who secretly gives information about someone to the police.

70 **candidate** (page 59)

one of the people who is competing in an election or competing for a job.

71 **Nobel Peace Prize** (page 59)

an international prize given each year for work towards world peace.

72 **widow** (page 61)

a woman whose husband has died.

73 **resigned** – *to resign* (page 62)

to state formally that you are leaving your job.

74 **retired** – *to retire* (page 62)

the time after you permanently stop working, or the act of permanently stopping work.

Dictionary extracts adapted from the Macmillan English Dictionary © Macmillan Publishers Ltd 2002.

Exercises

People in the story

The following people are in Nelson Mandela's story. Write a name next to a description below.

FW de Klerk   Winnie Mandela   ~~Gadla~~   Evelyn
Graça Machel   Oliver Tambo   Steve Biko   Robert Sobukwe
Walter Sisulu   Jongintaba   Zeni   Botha

1	Gadla	Nelson Mandela's father.
2		Nelson Mandela's first wife.
3		Nelson Mandela's second wife, who went to prison in 1991.
4		South Africa's new leader in 1989, who worked with Mandela to end apartheid.
5 6		Mandela's friends, who also worked in law and were involved in the ANC. (2 people)
7		The president of the South African Students' Organisation who was beaten to death by the police in 1973.
8		The creator of the Pan African Congress, who started the anti-pass campaign.
9		Nelson Mandela's third wife.
10		King of the Thembu tribe, who organised Mandela's education.
11		One of Mandela's daughters from his second marriage, who he did not see for 20 years.
12		The president who first offered to free Mandela in 1985.

Background information

Choose the correct information to complete the sentences.

1 The first Europeans to come to live in South Africa were
  (the Dutch) / the English.

2 These first Europeans came to South Africa a few hundred / thousand
  years before Mandela was born.

3 When the first Europeans came, the majority of people living in South
  Africa were black / white.

4 The Dutch Boers made the Africans / English work for them as slaves.

5 Thousands of Zulus / Boers were killed at Blood River as the Boers tried
  to move north.

6 The British and the Boers fought two wars before / after diamonds and
  gold were found in South Africa.

7 In 1910, South Africa became a union and a part of the
  British / Dutch Empire.

8 The African National Congress was created in 1912 / 1944.

True or false?

Read the statements about Nelson Mandela. Write T (True) or F (False).

1 When Mandela was born, the apartheid system did not yet exist in South Africa.	F
2 Mandela's father always obeyed the white leaders.	
3 Mandela's first job was as a lawyer.	
4 Mandela wanted the white people to leave South Africa.	
5 Mandela took some ideas of peaceful protest from Ghandi in India.	
6 Mandela was always against using illegal forms of protest.	
7 Mandela became known around the world for his speeches during the Treason Trial.	

8 Mandela was found guilty at the end of the Treason Trial and sent to prison.	
9 Mandela did not defend himself in his second trial.	
10 Mandela had no contact with his family during his time in prison.	
11 Mandela made plans for the future when he was in prison.	
12 Mandela accepted Botha's offer of freedom from prison.	
13 Mandela spent 27 years in prison.	
14 Mandela became president of South Africa immediately after leaving prison.	
15 Mandela retired from his job as president when he was 85.	

Vocabulary: people

There are many nouns in the story which are types of people. Complete the sentences with one of these words from the box.

> bride   chief   widow   clients   members   ancestors
> president   nephew   ~~slaves~~   stranger

1 Some Europeans who arrived in South Africa made Africans work for them as ....*slaves*........ with no pay.

2 Jongintaba paid the family of a woman who was going to marry Nelson, but Nelson did not want her to be his ....

3 Nelson believed that it was wrong to marry someone you did not know, someone who was a ....

4 Gadla, as .... , was the most important man in his village and tribe.

5 Gadla's .... was Jongintaba, the son of his brother or sister.

6 The most powerful politician in a country who has won the election is the ....

73

7 Many black people who were unhappy with the situation in South Africa became .... of the ANC, to try to fight for change.

8 Black South Africans knew that they should have freedom because their .... had already lived in the country for many years before the Europeans arrived.

9 Nelson and Oliver's law firm had many black .... who needed legal help.

10 Graça Machel's first husband had already died when she met Nelson. She was a ....

Vocabulary: law and rights

Change the order of the letters in brackets to make words related to law and rights. The first one is an example.

1 The ANC wanted black people to have the same .... *rights* .... (grhsti) as whites, for example to be able to vote.

2 After the Defiance Campaign, the police .... (sderarte) many of the ANC leaders.

3 Nelson studied law at university and became a .... (yrawle) after that.

4 Mandela and the other ANC leaders were on .... (lrita) to see if they were innocent or .... (lutgyi) of the crime.

5 The most important person in the court, the .... (deguj), decided that they had not committed any crime.

6 If someone committed the crime of treason, their .... (thupsenimn) might be death.

7 When their legal protest did not work, the ANC decided to .... (arekb) the law and use illegal methods.

8 When he was in court in 1963, Mandela refused to .... (fddeen) himself. He talked about the terrible life of the blacks in South Africa instead.

9 In 1963, Mandela was found guilty of the crime and .... (cdesetnen) to life in prison.

10 As the white government became more worried about the ANC, they
.... (spades) more laws against black people. For example,
blacks were not .... (dawloel) to stay in hotels or walk
through doors for white people.

11 Nelson Mandela wanted blacks to have the same rights as whites. He
was fighting for .... (qaelu) rights for everybody.

12 After the Defiance Campaign, the Government ....
(andenb) ANC leaders from having meetings or belonging to any
organisation.

Grammar: *had to / couldn't*

**Complete the sentences with *had to* or *couldn't* to describe obligations
and what was not allowed.**

During apartheid, black South Africans:

1 ....*couldn't*........ vote.
2 .... carry their passbooks with them.
3 .... walk on the street after 11 p.m.
4 .... live in the townships.
5 .... work.
6 .... travel freely around the country.
7 .... go to a white-only beach.
8 .... obey apartheid laws.

After the Defiance Campaign, the ANC leaders were freed from prison.
But they:

9 .... speak to the media.
10 .... travel where they wanted.
11 .... be careful.
12 .... work secretly.
13 .... go into an airport.
14 .... take part in meetings.

75

In Robben Island prison, Nelson Mandela:

15 .... write more than two letters a year.

16 .... have visits from his children.

17 .... get special permission for his wife's visits.

18 .... leave to go to his son's funeral.

19 .... work outside in the rain in winter.

20 .... speak to other prisoners at the beginning.

21 .... try to have hope for the future.

22 .... often get news from the outside world.

Sentence transformations: obligation and permission

Rewrite the sentences using the words in capitals. The first one is an example.

1 It was impossible for black South Africans to live where they wanted. (COULD) Black South Africans ..... *could not live where they wanted* .....

2 It was not possible for children to visit prisoners in Robben Island prison. (ALLOWED)
Children ....

3 The ANC leaders could not meet freely after their arrest. (BANNED)
The ANC leaders ....

4 Winnie Mandela couldn't leave her house when she was under house arrest. (HAD)
Winnie Mandela ....

5 After 1978, the Government said that the blacks could own property in the townships. (LET)
After 1978, the Government ....

6 Nelson Mandela put pressure on the Government to give equal rights to black South Africans. (MADE)
Nelson Mandela ....

7 Americans were not allowed to invest money in South Africa. (ILLEGAL) It ....

8 Journalists could not report the news freely. (POSSIBLE)
   It ....
9 It was necessary for the situation in South Africa to change. (HAD)
   The situation in South Africa ....
10 The Government said that the blacks had to go to the tribal
   homelands. (MADE)
   The Government ....

Grammar: comparatives

Complete the sentences using a comparative form of the adjective in brackets (eg more/less + adjective, adjective + -er, etc).

1 When the Government wanted to work with Nelson Mandela, his life
   in prison became .... *easier* .... (easy).
2 Conditions at Mandela's second prison, Pollsmoor, were
   .... (good) than at Robben Island. There was a library
   and a radio.
3 As more and more apartheid laws were passed in the 1950s, life became
   .... (difficult) for black South Africans.
4 Mandela's health was getting .... (bad) and the
   government was worried that their best hope for change might die.
5 When peaceful protest did not work, the ANC leaders agreed to use
   .... (violent) methods.
6 Because of the terrible conditions in the townships, the blacks became
   .... (angry).
7 The new laws which the Government passed after the Defiance
   Campaign made it .... (easy) for the ANC leaders to
   meet and continue action.
8 The new South Africa, with Nelson Mandela as president, has become
   a .... (peaceful) place.

Grammar: *too much / many, not enough*

Complete the following sentences with *too much, too many* or *not enough*.

1 The ANC felt that .... *not enough* .... political prisoners were freed by the Government. They believed that the Government should free all of them.

2 There was .... space to move freely in Nelson's small prison cell.

3 Nelson spent .... time in prison – he was a freedom fighter, not a criminal.

4 Many new, young ANC members in the 1940s felt the ANC was less strong than in the 1930s. They said there was .... talking and .... action – they wanted to fight harder.

5 Conditions in the townships were terrible: there was .... unemployment, ... disease and .... problems with the police.

Word focus: compound nouns

a Join words from the two columns to make compound nouns from the story.

1	political...	gas
2	war...	station
3	tear...	zone
4	prison...	line
5	power...	cell
6	phone...	firm
7	gold...	mine
8	law...	prisoner

b   **Complete the gaps with one of the compound nouns from the table, in singular or plural form.**

1   Electricity is made in a ....

2   Mandela's first job was in a ....

3   Mandela graduated and then started a .... to help black clients who needed legal help.

4   The ANC wanted all ...... *political prisoners* ...... to be freed, including terrorists.

5   The police used .... to get the black protesters off the streets.

6   The Spear of the Nation attacked .... to make it difficult for the Government's communication system to work.

7   Mandela spent a long time in his small .... and was not allowed to speak to other prisoners.

8   With violent protests, fighting and terrorism, South Africa was quickly becoming a ....

Vocabulary: verbs

Choose the correct verb to complete the sentences. All the expressions are used in the story.

1   Nelson worked in Johannesburg so that he could take / earn / give / win enough money to live.

2   Nelson made / did / gave / decided the decision to leave Mqhekezweni and go to Johannesburg.

3   Nelson made / built / packed / did a case and left for Johannesburg.

4   Winnie's father was worried that Winnie was doing / having / taking / making a mistake when she married Nelson.

5   In Johannesburg, Nelson quickly got / made / had / knew friends with members of the ANC who wanted to change the lives of black people.

6   Mandela said that the Government had to take / keep / listen / have its promises to free prisoners and give equal rights to black people.

Published by Macmillan Heinemann ELT
Between Towns Road, Oxford OX4 3PP
A division of Macmillan Publishers Limited
Companies and representatives throughout the world
Heinemann is the registered trademark of Pearson Education, used under licence.

ISBN 978–0–2307–3117–2
ISBN 978–0–2307–1659–9 (with CD edition)

First published 2009
Text © Macmillan Publishers Limited 2009
Design and illustration © Macmillan Publishers Limited 2009
This version first published 2009

All rights reserved; no part of this publication may be reproduced, stored in a
retrieval system, transmitted in any form, or by any means, electronic,
mechanical, photocopying, recording, or otherwise, without the prior written
permission of the publishers.

Illustrated by Peter Harper
Cover photograph by Getty/Tom Stoddart

The authors and publishers would like to thank the following for permission
to reproduce their photographic material:
African Pictures/ Cedric Nunn p 17, African Pictures/ Oryx Media Archive
p 53; Getty/ AFP p 62, Getty/ Hulton Archive pp 6, 20, 46; Link Photo
Library/ BAHA p 37, Link Photo Library/ Jurgen Schadeberg p 16, Link
Photo Library/ Mayibuye pp 13, 24, 33, 41; News International Syndication/
The Times p 59; PA Photos/ Weitz AP p 54; Reuters/ Mike Hutchings p 44,
Reuters/ Radu Sigheti p 30, Reuters/ Russell Boyce p 56; Rex Features/ Nils
Jorgensen p 51.

Printed and bound in Thailand

2013 2012 2011
8   7   6   5   4

with CD edition

2013 2012 2011
8   7   6   5